GRACIE

Also by Joan MacLeod

Amigo's Blue Guitar
Another Home Invasion
Homechild
The Hope Slide / Little Sister
The Shape of a Girl / Jewel
The Valley
Toronto, Mississippi
2000

All available from Talonbooks

GRACIE

A Play

Joan MacLeod

Talonbooks

Talonbooks
278 East First Avenue, Vancouver, British Columbia, Canada V5T 1A6
www.talonbooks.com

First printing: 2018

Typeset in Arno
Printed and bound in Canada on 100% post-consumer recycled paper

Cover illustration by Dmitriy Morozov
Cover design by Chloë Filson
Interior design by Typesmith

Achy Breaky Heart (Don't Tell My Heart)
Words and Music by Don Von Tress
Copyright © 1991 UNIVERSAL –MILLHOUSE MUSIC
All Rights Reserved   Used by Permission
Reprinted by Permission of Hal Leonard LLC

Talonbooks acknowledges the financial support of the Canada Council for the Arts, the Government of Canada through the Canada Book Fund, and the Province of British Columbia through the British Columbia Arts Council and the Book Publishing Tax Credit.

Canada   Canada Council Conseil des arts for the Arts du Canada   BRITISH COLUMBIA   BRITISH COLUMBIA ARTS COUNCIL An agency of the Province of British Columbia

LIBRARY AND ARCHIVES CANADA CATALOGUING IN PUBLICATION

MacLeod, Joan, 1954–, author

    Gracie / a play by Joan MacLeod ; with an introduction by Marita Dachsel.

ISBN 978-1-77201-202-6 (SOFTCOVER)

    I. Dachsel, Marita, writer of introduction II. Title.

PS8575.L4645G73 2018   C812'.54   C2018-900752-4

For Ana Celeste

CONTENTS

INTRODUCTION

By Marita Dachsel

On opening night of the world premiere production of *Gracie*, when the lights came up on Lili Beaudoin, the actor who played Gracie, she was a revelation. In her pouffed hair and pastel prairie dress, she embodied the young women of the Fundamentalist Church of Jesus Christ of Latter-Day Saints (FLDS) who are seen in photographs from Bountiful, British Columbia; Colorado City, Arizona; Hildale, Utah; and Yearning for Zion Ranch near Eldorado, Texas. Through great craft and talent, Beaudoin aged from an eight-year-old girl to a fifteen-year-old. She manifested the wonder, stubbornness, joy, confusion, and love that were specific to Gracie yet are recognizable in all children.

Many of us will see ourselves in Gracie's coming-of-age tale. There is something universal in her awakenings to the world around her, her burgeoning and confusing curiosities, her betrayals and losses. She is, after all, just a girl growing up.

But Gracie is a girl growing up in a society that's wildly different from that of the majority of the population, and consequently her opportunities, choices, and worldview differ from most of ours.

Gracie belongs to a Mormon fundamentalist family and community, one that closely resembles FLDS, which is just one of many varied Mormon fundamentalist sects. The lives of Mormon fundamentalists who live in Bountiful and multiple communities in the United States differ in various ways from mainstream Mormons and from the general public, but it's their doctrine of polygamy that sets them outside societal norms.

While the mainstream Mormon Church (the Church of Jesus Christ of Latter-day Saints, or LDS) has distanced itself from Mormon fundamentalism, largely thanks to polygamy, they share the same historical foundation; polygamous marriage – also known as plural or, historically, celestial marriage – was an important tenet of their faith. (It is worth noting that mainstream Mormonism continues to permit polygamy in the afterlife. The current president of the LDS, Russell M. Nelson, is officially sealed – married "in time and eternity" – to two women, his late wife and his current wife; according to Mormon theology, he will be polygamous in the afterlife.)

Joseph Smith founded the church in 1830. It claims to be the restoration of the original church of Jesus Christ and has reinstated various doctrines that Smith and his followers believed to be practiced during the "golden age" when God communed directly with humans. Among the many revelations Smith received from God, one was an instruction, in the mid-1830s, to restore plural marriage. He tentatively, secretly attempted to reinstate celestial marriage a few times in the late 1830s, but in the early 1840s he introduced it to some of his closest friends. While we might never know the true number, it is believed that by 1844 Smith had married at least thirty-three women, and none, except his first wife Emma, lived with him publicly as wives. Of the women he married, some were already married to other men, some were sisters, two were mother and daughter, and some were teenagers. Smith married his good friend's fourteen-year-old daughter, and this practice continues today in some communities. While the most scandalous cases of twelve-year-old girls being "sealed" to church leaders are relatively rare, marriages between girls aged fourteen to eighteen to men two to three or even four times their age have been commonplace in Mormon fundamentalist communities.

After Smith's death, Brigham Young took control of the church and led the Latter-day Saints out west to settle in what would become Utah. There, plural marriage was widely and openly practiced until 1890, when the fourth leader of the church, President Wilford Woodruff, received his own revelation that plural marriages were no longer commanded by God. Church leaders continued to perform plural marriages in secret until 1904, when another revelation and the Second Manifesto stopped it. The practice was forced further underground.

In the 1920s, Mormon polygamists began to find each other. A group formed the "Council of Seven Friends" and claimed authority over the leader of the Mormon Church. Most contemporary Mormon fundamentalist groups can trace their origin to these men, including the FLDS group in Bountiful, B.C.

Because polygamy is a crime in both Canada and the United States, it's impossible to know precisely how many Mormon fundamentalists there are today. Estimates place between 15,000 and 22,000 polygamists within organized groups and with up to 15,000 independents. It's easy to see them as a homogenous group, but their beliefs and cultures can vary dramatically.

The sect that Gracie belongs to practices the law of placing, in which young women are told by church leadership whom they are to marry through divine authority. These "placements," like many aspects of community life, reward the older, more powerful men. In Gracie's community, girls are married off and impregnated as soon as possible, and the young men are made to either leave the community or accept being overworked for little pay in hopes of gaining favour – and a wife – from church leadership. Perhaps it's because Canada prides itself on religious freedom (and upholding Pierre Elliot Trudeau's assertion that "there's no place for the state in the bedrooms of the nation") that the community of Bountiful has mostly been ignored by authorities, which have allowed these marriages to happen. This changed in the mid-2000s, when some of the horrors committed by Warren Jeffs, the FLDS leader based in America, were discovered. (He is now in jail, having been sentenced to life plus twenty years, and continues from prison to lead a faction of the church.) In July 2017, two prominent leaders in Bountiful were tried and found guilty of polygamy: James Oler with five wives, and Winston Blackmore with at least twenty-four. Blackmore has styled himself as a kinder, more progressive polygamist – for example, his wives and children don't wear the pastel prairie dresses so associated with the FLDS – but how progressive is a man who, by many accounts, has fathered more than 145 children?

It's hard to describe the love I felt for Gracie as she came alive on opening night. I wanted to care for her, comfort her, protect her. I could not help but remember how our fates are tied to our opportunities, and Gracie's were limited: marry and mother young, or be banished – leave her family and the only life she knows behind. Neither seemed fair.

Bountiful is the face of polygamy in our country, but it's important to remember that not all polygamy has Mormon roots, and not all polygamy relies on child brides. Plural marriage will continue regardless of legislation, but we can and must work harder to protect children like Gracie.

Sources and Further Reading

Adams, Brooke. "LDS splinter groups growing."
  The Salt Lake Tribune. August 9, 2005. Accessed
  February 2018. http://archive.sltrib.com/story
  .php?ref=%2Futah%2Fci_2925222.

Canada. "Offences Against Conjugal Rights" (§290–293)
  and "Unlawful Solemnization of Marriage"
  (§294–295). *Criminal Code of Canada.* February 8,
  2018. Accessed February 2018. http://laws-lois.justice
  .gc.ca/eng/acts/C-46/page-71.html#h-88.

Church of Jesus Christ of Latter-day Saints, The. "Official
  Declaration 1." *The Church of Jesus Christ of Latter-day
  Saints.* Accessed February 2018. https://www.lds.org
  /scriptures/dc-testament/od/1.

Lak, Daniel. "Canada's polygamy legislation." *CBC News.*
  November 23, 2011. Accessed February 2018.
  http://www.cbc.ca/news/canada/canada-s
  -polygamy-legislation-1.856477.

O'Neill, Ann. "FLDS prophet Warren Jeffs still rules his
  flock." *CNN.* August 8, 2016. Accessed February 2018.
  https://www.cnn.com/2016/08/08/us/flds-warren
  -jeffs/index.html.

PLAYWRIGHT'S NOTE

This play is a work of fiction inspired by Fundamentalist Church of Jesus Christ of Latter-Day Saints (FLDS) communities in Canada and the United States. Gracie and all other characters and events mentioned in the play are fictional.

PRODUCTION HISTORY

Gracie was first produced from January 20 to February 19, 2017, at the Belfry Theatre in Victoria, British Columbia, with the following cast and crew:

GRACIE: Lili Beaudoin

Director: Vanessa Porteous
Set and Costume Designer: Catherine Hahn
Lighting Designer: Narda McCarroll
Composer and Sound Designer: Tobin Stokes
Stage Manager: Jennifer Swan
Apprentice Stage Manager (Belfry Theatre): Sadie Fox
Apprentice Stage Manager (Alberta Theatre Projects):
    Meredith Johnson

Gracie was remounted from February 28 to March 18, 2017, by Alberta Theatre Projects at the Martha Cohen Theatre in Calgary, Alberta, with nearly the same cast and crew.

PRODUCTION NOTE

Gracie is fifteen years old. She wears a dirty, ankle-length, cotton, print dress, running shoes, and her hair pulled back from her face in a long braid that is growing ragged. Gracie's accent diminishes as she grows older but it never quite leaves her. There are many suggested locations, but the fitting room is key. Events occur from 2000 through 2007.

Because of the multiple locations and time shifts, and because Gracie never leaves the stage, this isn't a prop-heavy play. Aspects of the setting – like weather and the season – can be established with music, lighting, etc.

CHARACTERS

GRACIE, who gives voice to multiple characters
     (in order of appearance):
MUMMA
SHELBY
ALLIE
MARIE
CELESTE
RITA
TEACHER
BILLY
BRANDON
BLACK-HAIRED GIRL
MARIAH
BOY
NURSE
WALMART CLERK

DESIGN NOTE

Gracie is both narrator and voiced character in this play. Gracie's narrations are displayed in roman text, and her voiced dialogue is displayed in indented, *italic* text. All other characters – all of whom are also voiced by Gracie – are preceded by parentheses that display their names.

Part One

Lights up.
GRACIE is eight years old, sitting
in the van. It's spring.

Mumma drives. Billy's got the map. Celeste, then me, then
Marie, in the back. I never get my turn up front or at the
window neither. I got the cooler under my feet. It isn't a
good place to sit. I got purple alphabet letters, made out of
macaroni, that spell out my name. *G-R-A-C-I-E.* I play with
them inside my pocket, trying to guess what letter is what.
No one even knows I got them letters. They make my hands
smell like blueberries. Like candy.

When it gets dark, we quit driving. We sleep in tents.
Mumma and Marie in one tent; Celeste and me in the other.
Billy sleeps in the van to make sure no one steals it. The
rule in the tent is not to touch the sides because it's raining.
But I roll too far and get us wet in the middle of the night.
Celeste is so mad she won't speak to me. Mumma says that
something someone does in their sleep isn't their fault and
for Celeste to grow up. She's sixteen years old.

We have cereal in its own little box for breakfast,
sandwiches for lunch and dinner. We have muffins to share
in Bonners Ferry. That's the name of a town near the border.
We don't see no ferry.

Mumma tells the man at the border we're coming to
Canada for a wedding. She don't tell him she's the one getting
married. She don't say we're gonna live there and she'd told
us not to say so neither.

Deer crossing. Elk crossing. Kilometre this and kilometre that ...

Mumma slows down. We finally stop moving. There's a chain across the road, right in front of us. A sign with a big X hanging from that chain. Mumma shuts the engine off.

We're here.

A long house, two stories tall. Two big barns and lots of little houses. Trailers, big and little, up against the mountain. We sit forever, waiting for someone to come let us in. It looks like we froze. Maybe we have froze. Canada is just as cold as everyone says.

Marie pokes me in the side. Two big boys on dirt bikes have shown up behind that chain. Then big girls carrying babies.

Mumma, bikes ...

All sorts of bikes. And all sorts of kids riding them bikes. Trikes too. Then kids on horses. And little kids on ponies.

Even the babies are staring at us. Maybe they've never seen a van like ours before. Maybe they don't have vans in Canada. Maybe all they got is horses and bikes. I don't know what they have here. I only been here ten minutes.

One of the big boys revs up his dirt bike. He comes down the side of the road, around that chain and sprays up mud when he stops. Then he raps on the window where Celeste's sitting. Mumma tells her to wave hello but she won't do it. Celeste didn't want to come here. I didn't want to come here neither. But Celeste had to leave behind more friends than me, so she thinks she's got it worse.

Mumma gives a little wave to the man walking toward us.

(*as* MUMMA) That's him. You call him Mr. Shelby until he tells you different.

He's fat and holding hands with two women. There're more women walking behind. He's old but not real old – just like Mumma said he'd be. He puts a key in a lock and the chain falls down. Mumma gets out of the van and Mr. Shelby takes off his ball cap. They hug each other.

We line up. He shakes Billy's hand, then Celeste's and Marie's.

He pats me on the top of my head. He calls me "little Gracie." He wants to know if I had a good trip.

I tell him about sitting in the middle. I tell him about the cooler.

He says that if I need anything to let him know.

I need a bike.

Mumma pinches me on my shoulder.

I need a bike, please.

Mumma says I don't need a thing.

He shows Billy where to park our van. Mr. Shelby puts the chain back up. He holds out his hand for me to take. Mumma gives me a little shove. I take his hand.

Now everyone walks behind me and him. Even Mumma and them.

(*as* SHELBY) How're you doing, Gracie?

Good.

Except I'm not really. I'm sad and lonesome for my old bike.

We stop walking. His hand goes back on top of my head.

(*as* SHELBY) I want you to be happy here. You can come talk to me if you're feeling troubled. Any time.

He turns around to talk to Mumma and them now too.

(*as* SHELBY) Welcome to your new home.

It's two houses stuck together. Another family lives on the other side. There's a porch across the front of both places. Marie's pouting that Mr. Shelby made friends with me before her. Mumma lets Marie go in first. I go next.

There's a rocking chair and a couch. A little kitchen – table and chairs. We got our own toilet and that too. Marie and me have our own bedroom. Just us two – in one room. And Mumma and Celeste got a whole room just for them.

Our old bedroom? It was big as a barn, full of bunk beds and kids. All I had that was my own was my drawer. *G-R-A-C-I-E* glued to the front in macaroni. When Mumma said we had to move I wanted to take my drawer with me. But she put her foot down.

(*as* MUMMA) Only take what's in it.

So I did. Then I chipped off them letters and coloured them with blueberry marker. That isn't stealing. Whatever girl come there next will have her own name to put on that drawer.

We put away our things. I have two drawers in the dresser here except I don't have nothing yet to put in the bottom drawer.

Billy gets set up in a trailer, down on the other side of the chain, with a boy called Brandon. They got the biggest microwave oven you've ever seen. I never lived somewhere different than Billy.

Beat.

A tall girl comes out on the porch from next door. She says she's in grade four. She wants to know what grade I'm in. I don't say nothing. I don't know what grade I'm in. I never been to school. We learned at home. She hands me a plastic bag. There's a doll inside. It used to be hers but she don't play with dolls no more. She'd rather ride horses. The doll looks like a real baby. The girl called her Tanya but she says I can call her anything I want.

I go back in the house. I put the doll in my bottom drawer. I close it up careful. The girl follows me in.

(*as ALLIE*) Don't you like her?

I love her. I love Tanya. I never had a doll.

She says if I take Tanya out of the drawer that she'll show me how to feed her. The girl's name is Allie. I tell her who I am. I take Tanya out and put her on the bed.

(*as ALLIE*) You should lay her down on her back. Not on her face.

I feel terrible that I already done something bad to Tanya. Allie picks Tanya up.

(*as ALLIE*) Babies are born face down. Did you know that?

No.

(*as ALLIE*) My mom's a midwife. I'm going to be a midwife too.

Allie takes a little bottle filled with water from her pocket and puts it in Tanya's mouth.

(*as ALLIE*) When mothers are having their babies they leave their bodies. They float up above their pain.

Like angels ...

(*as ALLIE*) No! Because it hurts! It's unbearable!

She pulls Tanya's dress up. There's a facecloth diaper inside Tanya's underpants.

(*as ALLIE*) Look.

And a little pipe between her legs where the water from the bottle comes out.
Before she leaves we put a towel in the drawer for Tanya.

(*as ALLIE*) Watch this.

Allie lays Tanya down on her back ... and just like that Tanya's eyes shut tight.

(*as ALLIE*) She's sound asleep.

That night I'm so excited about Tanya I can't sleep. I keep climbing over Marie and opening the drawer to check on her.

Marie says that if I do that one more time she's going to throw Tanya out the window. She would too. Mumma hollers for us to stop talking. We've got a big day tomorrow.

Bells ring.

Mumma puts on her special garments. She puts on her dress. I wear my good blue dress and Marie and Celeste put on their blue dresses too. Mumma has a white shirt all pressed for Billy. She brushes out my hair. Then she starts in on hers.

We go to the hall. Mumma and Mr. Shelby have their ceremony. They are joined now for eternity. And we're joined to him for eternity now too. We go down in the basement after; there's a big lunch spread out. Everything's nice and everyone is nice to us.

Beat.

The next day there's a brand new bike on the porch. I think it belongs to Allie and them next door, but Mumma says it's mine. The bike is purple with gold streamers. Thank you, Jesus. Thank you, Mr. Shelby. Thank you, Canadian Tire. I love you bike. I ride up and down the lanes past the houses and trailers. I ride by the mill where Billy works. He's out in the yard, stacking posts. He whistles at me and my bike. I ride 'til dark every day.

Beat.

I thought we were going to town today.

Mumma says not today. She braids Celeste's hair. She rats it up high in front and sprays it in place.
    Now Mumma shows her how to put on lipstick. Celeste says she don't want to wear lipstick.

I will.

Mumma's not paying attention to me. She's ironing our blue dresses.

(*as MARIE*) Look …

Marie points to the other bedroom. There are special garments laid out on Celeste's bed. There's a dress hanging by the window.

I didn't know you were getting married too.

Celeste says that she knew. She heard Mumma talking on the phone to Mr. Shelby before we come.

(*as CELESTE*) They made a deal.

Bells ring.

Celeste marries the boy on the dirt bike. His name is Jamie.
He's Mr. Shelby's oldest boy. That night there's a dinner at the
big house with singing and speeches. Everyone says they're a
beautiful couple even though Celeste just looks grumpy. Jamie's
got black hair and blue eyes. He's got a brand new house, just
down the lane from ours, looking right at the mountain.

But Celeste won't stay with him in that house. Not even
one day married and she's back at our house first thing.

Mumma puts her arm around Celeste.

(*as MUMMA*) You're someone's wife now. A first wife. To a
first son. That's an honour.

Celeste don't care who Jamie is. She don't like what he tried
to do to her in the middle of the night.

Maybe your husband was asleep when he done what he done.
Maybe it wasn't his fault.

Celeste tells me to shut up.

(*as MUMMA*) Back to your house, right this minute!

Mumma goes into her bedroom. Celeste goes out the door.
Mumma hollers for Marie and me to watch out on the porch
to make sure Celeste goes back in her house. Celeste stands
out there in front. Her house is nice. It's made out of logs.

It even smells nice. Jamie is nice too. He likes the way
I ride my bike. "Racie Gracie." That's what he calls me.
Marie says Celeste is just spoiled. She's used to getting what
she wants all the time. If Marie was married to Jamie she
wouldn't run home to Mumma.

Me neither.

Celeste's still out on the stoop. She blows her nose, then pushes open the door.

Mumma! She's gone back in.

I go out on my bike. I ride down to the chain. I spray up some dirt when I stop, with the back tire – just like Jamie done with his dirt bike.

I lean my bike against the post and walk around to the other side of the chain. There's a valley out front that goes on and on. At first I think it's covered in snow. It's not snow … It's cherry blossoms. I thought Canada was going to be a big lake. I don't know who told me that – but they were wrong. There's more to it than that.

I turn around and look at the sign with the *X*. "No trespassing" in big black letters underneath. It's the same here as where we lived before. I know I'm home when I see that sign. I go back around the post, on the right side of the sign, back to where I'm supposed to be. I make eight marks in the dirt because I am eight years old.

Mumma said to say we were born in Canada, if anyone we don't know asks where we're from.

My name is Gracie Lorraine Shelby! I was born in the valley of Canada. A valley of bikes and horses and dolls. I was born into a big and beautiful family. A family that loves God and loves each other.

Blackout.

Function of the
P.O.V

Part Two

*GRACIE is nine years old. It's
early morning, winter.
GRACIE wakes to the sound of an
airtight woodstove opening.*

Mumma stirs up the coals. She puts in more wood. I look
into the dark to see how much snow come in the night. Lots.
Marie keeps snoring. I climb over her and she snores through
that too.

   I get into bed with Mumma. We don't have to get up
for prayers until the house gets warm. She nurses my baby
brother Justin. He's a wild little thing. He makes Mumma
tired. On a good day he falls back asleep after he's been filled
up with milk. I pick him up careful, just like Mumma taught
me. I lay him in his cradle, on his back, so that Mumma don't
have to get out of bed. Then I climb back in with her.

Bells ring.

The bells wake Marie up too. I put a blanket on the floor,
in front of the airtight. We get down on our knees and start
our morning prayers.

   Allie comes at seven. We tuck our dresses into our snow
pants, put on our boots and parkas. Allie and me got little
flashlights that strap onto our heads that Mr. Shelby gave all
of us at Christmas.

We hold hands, walking through the snow to the big
house. On the way we choose which house we want to live in
when we're grown up. We plan out what colour we'll paint it.

Allie wants a pink house and a Ford-150 pickup. I want a
pink house too. And an Aerostar van. We like making plans,
me and Allie.

(*as* RITA) Don't bring the cold in with you!

Mumma's sister wives Rita and Kathleen are in charge of
breakfast.

Allie and me and eight other girls are helpers today.
We put plates and that around all the tables. A warm bun and
a piece of bacon on each plate, and then two orange slices.
We make sure there's a juice glass at every place, a jug at every
table. We fill up the glasses where the little kids sit.

Bells ring.

At eight o'clock over a hundred boys and girls come in.
Mr. Shelby says a prayer before we eat. Then he says,

(*as* SHELBY) Good day, children!

And we say "Good day!" right back to him. He tells us God
loves us and he loves us too. Each and every one.

Our school is beside the hall. Allie and me don't walk to
school together. She goes with a group of girls who are in the
five/six split with her. I should be in that class too but I had a
hard time last year when we first come. I'm still in grade four.
I was behind in reading. I couldn't do arithmetic at all. Marie

and me got teased for how we talk and where we come from. They're used to us now.

I did go see Mr. Shelby, just like he said I could, if I was feeling troubled. I told him that I was troubled to still be in grade four and that it was arithmetic that was troubling me most of all. So maybe I should do something else.

He said it's important to learn arithmetic. And that maybe I'm having a hard time because where I lived before I didn't have nothing much to count. He winked at me.

(*as* SHELBY) But now you can count your blessings.

I do count my blessings. I love Reading and Social Studies and Science. I love Art and P.E. I love everything except arithmetic.

He patted me on my head.

(*as* SHELBY) Gracie, you're full of beans.

Beat.

In Social Studies we work on our Men from History posters. Half of us gets Joseph Smith and the other half gets Jesus. We didn't get to choose our groups. If we did I would've chosen Jesus. I love Joseph Smith too but I really, really love Jesus.

I cut out an old-time drawing of Joseph and the golden plates. They're not plates from the cupboard. They're like a big book made of stone and lights. He has dark hair and bright eyes like Celeste's husband Jamie.

We learn more about how Joseph Smith was murdered by an angry mob. Some kids start crying. Teacher says not to cry.

(*as* TEACHER) He'll be a God in the celestial kingdom. And for that we should all be happy.

She comes over to look at the angry mob I drew for my poster. I wanted the mob to look like a tornado.

(*as* TEACHER) That looks like scribbling.

I almost start crying too, except Teacher turns nice again. She lets us eat our snack early so that we can think about how it will be for all of us in eternity – what a good time we're going to have when we get there, if we keep being nice.

After school, I help Celeste.

(*as* CELESTE) Easy does it, fatso.

Celeste picks up Roberta and puts her in the kitchen sink. Roberta loves her bath. I love being her auntie. She's younger than our brother Justin, but she's way bigger than him. She's nicer than him too. I put my hand on her back to make sure she don't tip over. She splashes water on me. She thinks that's funny.

Celeste likes being married now that she has Roberta.

Beat.

Billy comes by, just before we're going to bed.

Mumma says his hair is looking scraggly. She wants
to cut it.

He likes it the way it is.

She says not to talk back. He says that's not what
he's doing.

(*as* BILLY) Guys from town, with no experience – they're
getting paid twice as much as me for doing the same job. Plus
half my paycheque goes to rent for that old fall-down trailer.
Half the stuff in it don't even work. I was supposed to finish
high school. The school here doesn't go past grade ten. I'm
gonna talk to Shelby.

(*as* MUMMA) Don't you dare.

(*as* BILLY) Then you talk to him, Mumma. You're his wife.

(*as* MUMMA) No, sir.

(*as* BILLY) That's bullshit.

That's what Billy says. Right out loud to Mumma.

(*as* MUMMA) You girls go to bed – now.

We lie there, listening to Mumma reminding Billy how
Mr. Shelby saved our lives. How he gave us food and shelter
and love when no one else would.

Billy says us coming up here to Canada was all
about Celeste.

(*as* BILLY) She was the prize. They got pretty girls like her
going up and down that highway, night and day. And I'm

second prize. Cheap labour. Shelby don't care about anyone but himself.

Billy slams the door so hard the windows shake. That wakes up Justin and he starts to wail. Marie turns away and puts her pillow up around her ears. I warm Tanya up against my tummy.

There are thousands and thousands of spirits that are waiting to be born. Just a little while ago, Justin and Roberta were spirits. We can't see them. But I think about those spirits at night, up there in the dark, waiting to come down to earth.

Mumma soothes Justin. I worry about Billy, walking back home to his trailer, all alone.

There's a little ridge, down below the window, where I hide my old macaroni letters. I feel for one and pick it up careful with the end of my finger. G. G for "Gracie." G for "God." G for "Good." I put it back careful on the ridge. I'm finally getting sleepy. I put Tanya in her drawer.

Ssssshhhhh.

The house goes quiet again except for Marie's snoring. I like that sound. I need it to fall asleep.

Beat.

Billy is waiting for me when school's done. His hair, combed for the first time in a long time, tied back like a girl. He's got something he wants to show me. We walk past Celeste's house. She's taken Roberta to town today for her checkup.

We cut through some bushes, up a muddy path; we head up the mountain.

(*as* BILLY) You learning anything in school, Gracie?

I tell him about Social Studies and Joseph Smith.

(*as* BILLY) That's not what you're supposed to learn in Social Studies. What province do you live in?

British Columbia.

He asks me if I know what a province is.

(*as* BILLY) Gracie?

Something in books.

(*as* BILLY) We didn't live in a province before. We lived in one state and then another state.

No. We lived in a little house. Then we lived with Cyrus across the street.

(*as* BILLY) That's right. Our first house was in the state of Arizona. And right across the road, in Utah, was Cyrus's house.

Cyrus was an old man Mumma was assigned to before we come here. She married him when our daddy got kicked out. I was a baby then. Babies don't know much. I don't remember my daddy.

Cyrus had too many kids to count. He was always saying mixed-up things. He thought I was Celeste and Celeste was Marie. He couldn't even guess who Billy was. He was a nice old man. Then one day he got taken away and we come here.

(*as* BILLY) What country did we live in before? C'mon, Gracie.

I don't know. I don't care neither. Texas.

(*as* BILLY) Texas isn't a country. It's where our dad comes from.

We aren't supposed to talk about him. Mumma said. He ran over our dog on purpose. Sammy.

(*as* BILLY) There was more to it than that. You better not call old Shelby "Daddy."

He don't mind what I call him, long as I'm happy.

We cut through the bushes again and into a clearing. There's a big fallen tree that's made a shelter. Seats made of stumps and a little hubcap table. The branches from the tree make a roof.

I like it …

(*as* BILLY) It's my camp. There's even a bedroom.

Billy points to an old crib mattress. It's got a garbage bag for a blanket.

Can I bring Allie here the next time we come?

(*as* BILLY) This is between you and me. It's special.
Up here I don't have to listen to Brandon singing or playing video games.

I like it when Brandon sings.

(*as* BILLY) You watch yourself around Brandon ... I'm going to finish high school next month, at a night school in town. I already started studying. Getting a head start. It don't take a year to do a grade. Just a month or two.

Can I come and get done with grade four?

Billy says it's only for the higher grades. And that as soon as he's got his grade twelve he's going get a good job.

You have a good job. Mumma says you're making a big fuss over nothing.

Billy kicks at a chunk of ice until it busts open. Then he walks over and pulls on a rope, hanging from a tree.

(*as* BILLY) You still eat crackers?

There's a bag tied to the rope. He opens it up and pulls out another bag.

Goldfish ...

(*as* BILLY) You still like them best?

I love them.

We sit on stumps and eat the whole bag of Goldfish crackers. We pass a bottle of creek water back and forth. Then he asks me if I still love him.

Of course I do.

We make a plan to meet at the bottom of the path next week.

Beat.

I wait. And I wait some more. Billy doesn't come.

I walk out beyond the chain, to his trailer. It's falling down worse than before. Some of the windows are boarded up. I can hear Brandon inside, playing guitar. I knock on the door. The guitar stops.

(*as BRANDON*) Gracie! Come in, come in.

The trailer is dark inside even though it's sunny out. There are dirty dishes and empty beer bottles all over the counters.

Where's Billy?

(*as BRANDON*) Held up at work, I guess. You can visit me while you wait. Wanna hear a tune?

He plays "Achy Breaky Heart." He plays "House of the Rising Sun." He sings right to me. Like I'm the girl in the song.

Beat.

I have to go home.

I stand up. Brandon stands in front of me.

Billy says to watch you.

He says watch this. He puts his mouth on top of mine. His mouth tastes like Cheezies.

(*as* BRANDON) Was that your first kiss?

I don't say nothing. I run down the steps, all the way home.

Beat.

Mumma has her night with Mr. Shelby. We open the little door between Allie's side of the house and ours. Marie sleeps in Mumma's room to keep Justin company. It's lonesome in my room. I rub my hand along the ridge where my macaroni letters used to be. They got wet a couple of nights ago when the rain come in and turned to mush.

I get Tanya out of the drawer. We watch the rain on the window and look for the moon. I practice my reciting for Science class.

"This is the light of Christ. As also he is in the moon, and is the light of the moon, and the power thereof by which it was made ... As also he is the light of the stars ..."

Tonight there's no moon and stars for anyone to see. Just rain and dark.

Brandon's got dark eyes; they peek out at me from under his hair when he sings.

God doesn't talk to girls. But He listens. I pray for God to tell Mr. Shelby to find me a husband who's sweet and kind and not too old. Like Brandon. I put Tanya back in her drawer. When I turn around there is a face in the window, looking at me.

Beat.

Billy!

I unlatch the window and in he comes. He thinks coming through the window is funny. He's trying to talk in a whisper, but he don't whisper very good.

Beat.

You're drunk on beer.

He says you can't get drunk on beer. He's only had a few. He's come to say goodbye.

Where are you going?

(*as* BILLY) Back to the States.

What about night school?

He didn't have the right ID.

I don't want you to go anywhere.

(*as* BILLY) I know that. But I gotta get out of here soon as I can …

Then I notice a cut on the side of his face. His hands are cut up too. He won't say what happened. He wants to know if I have any money.

Why would I have money?

Billy knows all about Marie and me helping out with selling jam and honey this week in town.

Mumma takes the money. We don't even get to count it.

Mumma's not here tonight. He knows her schedule.

(*as* BILLY) You can show me where Mumma keeps her money.

She keeps it in her music box. In a little drawer with a little key. Except I don't tell him that.

You go on.

(*as* BILLY) Mumma used to say that to Sammy when he got in her way. I loved that little dog.

You go on or I'm calling Marie.

(*as* BILLY) Get me the money. Now. I mean it, Gracie.

He pulls on my braid. Hard.

   Don't!

He does it again.

   Marie!

Marie comes. Allie's mumma Mariah comes too.
We push Billy out the door into the rain. He calls us this.
He calls us that.

                    Beat.

In the morning I tell Mumma how Billy scared Marie and me.

   He pulled my hair.

She tells us to keep away from Billy. And that we're both
good girls.
   I go see Mr. Shelby. He says last night Billy smashed
up the trailer and got in a fight with Brandon – everybody
high on drugs. And that I'm not going to see Billy around
here anymore.

(*as* SHELBY) I know that will be hard. It might make you
sad. But God will give you strength, Gracie. He's watching
over you.

Marie asks Mumma where Billy's going to live. Mumma doesn't know. All she knows is that the path he's chosen isn't the righteous path. She don't know where it will take him.

Beat.

But I know what path he's on. I see him when I walk home from Celeste's, just before dark. I don't let him see me. Billy heads up to his camp, carrying bags of chips and big bottles of soda.

I see him head up that path every few days. Sometimes I think he sees me but he don't let on. Maybe he's still mad at me. He's dirtier every time I see him. That's for certain. He hardly looks like Billy.

Then I suppose he goes to the States or that. I don't see him no more. I don't know where he's gone.

Blackout.

Part Three

GRACIE is fourteen years old.
It's summer, morning.
We hear the sound of flowing water.
GRACIE is knee-deep in
the river. She sways.

"The earth rolls upon her wings, and the sun giveth his light by day, and the moon giveth her light by night, and the stars also give their light, as they roll upon their wings in their glory … Behold all these are kingdoms and any man who hath seen the least of these has seen God."

Allie's already up to her knees in the river. She holds her dress up high.

I can see your bee-hind!

(*as ALLIE*) Lucky you.

She's halfway across now. The water at her waist. She lets her dress float around her. It's eight o'clock and the sun's already hot and high.

Beat.

Now the water's flat where Allie used to be.

Lord in Heaven. Please, please, please …

Allie shoots back up. She hauls herself out of the water, just down the bank from me.

You scared me!

(*as* ALLIE) It's not my fault you don't know how to swim. How many times have I tried to teach you?

Mumma doesn't want us to swim.

Mumma thinks Allie's turned sassy. But I know she's brave. All week we've been riding our horses down to the flats by the river before it gets too hot. Pails for berries strapped to our saddles. Allie rides Dancer. He's big and mean. But Dancer doesn't scare her one bit. She shows him who's boss. I ride Triumph. He's a sweet old thing …
    Allie tries to wring out her dress.

That isn't going to work.

She sticks her tongue out at me and lies back on the grass.

I guess you don't mind being covered in mud neither.

(*as* ALLIE) You're a scaredy-cat, Gracie.

Good for me. (GRACIE *lies down on her back) Don't get me wet.*

We look for the angel Moroni in the clouds – his exquisite whiteness. We've been looking for him for years ... Sometimes we hold hands and reach up to the sky and practice for the exaltation – when the world will end and the righteous will all be raised to heaven.

Allie raises her knees. She arches her back, and huffs. She practices having a baby.

Beat.

Mumma made every sort of noise when my baby sister Emma was born. No time for the clinic or the hospital neither. Marie and Justin and me listen outside the door while Mumma screams. Mariah said Mumma could've died.

I shut my eyes. But the sunlight doesn't go away. And I feel God's presence again ...

"As also He is in the sun, and the light of the sun."

I could fall asleep in a heartbeat, but Allie pulls me up.

Just before home we see them, gathering across from the chain. They call themselves The Grannies – a bunch of old women from town who show up to protest when they got nothing better to do. They don't like the way we live – even though they don't know the first thing about us. We don't like them and the signs they march around with neither. We cross the road early and cut into the bush.

Beat.

Marie has her shift at the fruit stand in town this afternoon. Allie and me and Justin go with her. Marie drives like she's a hundred years old. Allie's got her Learner's. She'll have her real license in a few months and we'll drive ourselves to town then. We help box up the berries then leave Marie at the stand. We go do some shopping.

Justin's been asking for ice cream since we got here. Soon as we walk into the Dairy Queen it goes quiet, just for a moment. We're used to that. There're town girls at a booth in little shorts. A girl with black hair stares at us. I get Justin a cone. The air conditioning makes goose bumps underneath my dress.

Now they're all laughing at some big joke the black-haired girl said. Then she gets even louder; she looks straight at me and Allie.

(*as BLACK-HAIRED GIRL*) They live in the motel-house. One of them has sex with old Shelby, then an alarm goes off, and then he goes and has sex with the next mother in the next room. An hour later an alarm goes off and …

We try to get Justin to head for the door. He doesn't want to.

You're going or I'm taking your ice cream.

Soon as we're outside I hand back his ice cream; it falls over on the sidewalk. He's in tears now.

I'll get you a Popsicle at the pharmacy.

Justin hates Popsicles.

Then you're not getting anything.

Brandon is on the sidewalk outside the liquor store singing; he collects money in his guitar case. We don't talk to Brandon anymore; we haven't talked to him in years. Soon as he sees us he changes his tune.

(*as BRANDON, singing*) Don't tell my heart, my achy, breaky heart ...

I just don't think it'd understand ...

We cross the street. We sit on a bench up the next block, outside the bakery. A camper pulls up with some old people in it. They get out and take our picture, sitting there on the bench.
   All of a sudden Brandon is there, hollering.

(*as BRANDON*) Did you ask them if you could do that?

Allie and me look down at our hands.

(*as BRANDON*) Did you want her to take your picture?

We watch Justin watching the scene that Brandon's making.

(*as BRANDON*) Why don't you just "F" off!

The old people in the camper have had it with Brandon. They drive away, but Brandon isn't going anywhere.

(*as BRANDON*) How's things, Gracie?

He's thin as a post. Pale too ...

(*as BRANDON*) What's that? You too stuck up to talk to me? You don't want to hear about your own brother?

Brandon finally leaves; then he turns and yells back at us from the end of the block.

(*as BRANDON*) Last I heard Billy was in Vancouver turning tricks! Have a nice day!

Beat.

Allie reminds me that Brandon is going to hell.

(*as ALLIE*) Those Dairy Queen girls will be in hell for all eternity, too. A burden comes from being a chosen people.

I feel the blood pounding in my head. Then I'm on my feet.
   Brandon's sitting in front of the liquor store, tuning his guitar. He smiles at me in that secret way.
   I feel the Lord's spirit enter me.

GRACIE spits.

Brandon doesn't even flinch. He knows he deserves it.
   Justin's crying like the world's about to end.

I shouldn't have run away like that. I didn't mean to make you upset.

Allie says she's sorry about Billy.

The only brother I got is sitting right here.

I give Justin a big noisy kiss on his neck. It makes him laugh.
I promise to take him over to visit Roberta as soon as we're
back home.

Beat.

Celeste lets Roberta and Justin play with the ice-maker on
her fridge. Jamie-Junior's at our feet, making noise in his
playpen. An electric saw, down the hall, does its best to
drown him out.

It sounds like a war zone in here.

(*as* CELESTE) It is a war zone. Me and Jamie have been
fighting all week. He's building an addition.

You already got a big house.

(*as* CELESTE) Home renovation is a leading cause of divorce.
I read that in a magazine.

You shouldn't read those things.

(*as* CELESTE) I've been reading all sorts of stuff.

Beat.

Are you pregnant?

(*as* CELESTE) No. I thank Jesus and God both for that.

Celeste! Children are a blessing!

(*as* CELESTE) How'd you get so high and mighty, Gracie?

Beat.

Justin! Let's go.

He doesn't want to. Then stay right here! I'm sick of dragging you around all day!
　　Celeste tells me to sit back down.

I'm not high and mighty. Some days I'm just as mean as you.

Celeste thinks that's funny. She hauls out a book from inside her purse. The woman on the front wears a dress like what we wear.

(*as* CELESTE) She was married to Cyrus. Then she got assigned to his brother, the prophet. Neither one of them cared one bit about her. The more wives and kids the better their chance of becoming a God up there in Heaven. That's all she was. Something to give the men a better shot.

Celeste pushes the book right under my nose.

(*as* CELESTE) So she ran away and took her kids with her. Shelby's got eight wives ran away from him. Why do you suppose that is?

One was writing bad cheques. Mumma said.

(*as* CELESTE) Because that's what Shelby told her to say. Maybe I'll run away from Jamie.

Don't say that. You shouldn't be reading that neither.

(*as* CELESTE) Are you going to tell on me?

Maybe I will.

(*as* CELESTE) Mumma's the one should read this book ... She was Cyrus's twenty-third wife. With Shelby she's number eighteen. That's her idea of moving up in the world.

Don't make fun of Mumma ...

Celeste puts the book back in her purse. She picks up Jamie-Junior and gives him some ice to suck on.

(*as* CELESTE) He's teething. Our whole house is covered in drool. It's disgusting.

I'll give you a hand once Mumma's back on her feet –

And for a moment it looks like Celeste might cry.

Mumma's getting better. She's starting to bounce back. Don't worry about Mumma.

Beat.

That night Marie sleeps in Mumma's bed. They whisper half the night. I got Justin in with me. He takes up a lot of room for someone four years old.

It's dark and it's still too hot. The treetops make a zig-zag across the moon.

At Cyrus's the bunk beds were stacked up in threes. Marie and Celeste and me, we'd sit on the grass out front in a big circle of girls. In the middle of the circle – a cassette machine. We'd listen to the prophet on tape, telling us to "keep sweet."

I don't know what else he said. I just wanted to know whose turn it was to be in charge of the cassette machine.

Bells ring.

Marie marries Mr. Shelby's older brother. She's his seventh wife. He's foreman at the mill – Stanley. Marie doesn't complain once about marrying an old man. Mumma says she's proud of Marie. She's a good and righteous girl.

Bells ring.

Jamie takes a second wife. Amanda. Celeste doesn't need me anymore to help out with her kids. But we see Celeste even more than we did before. She keeps running back to our place, just like when she first got married.

(*as* CELESTE) Amanda don't do her share of the work. She thinks she's something special. Jamie thinks she's something special too.

Mumma puts her arm around Celeste.

(*as* MUMMA) When Grandma Lorraine had to make room for a second wife, she lay outside their bedroom and wept. But she came to love her sister wives, each and every one. In the celestial kingdom all your sorrows will fall away ... Trust the plan that God has made for you. It leads to eternity.

Beat.

Allie and me believe God has a plan for each of us. But we still like making our own plans too. Even if they're silly.

We'll be famous barrel-racers on the rodeo circuit. We'll go from town to town in our sparkly costumes and our silver Dodge Ram pickup with tinted windows and a camper on the back, our horse trailer in tow.

Or we'll be sister wives and live in a log house down by the river. We'll have six boys and six girls apiece.

Beat.

Or Allie will go to nursing school to be a midwife. I'll do the cooking and cleaning while she goes to school. We'll live in an apartment in Cranbrook or Calgary ... We even draw pictures of what our apartment might look like.

There'll be a bed come down from the wall and another bed in the corner that will have pillows for sitting on during the day. We make lists of all the things we'll have in our apartment. We even make a list of the food we'll have in the cupboard.

Beat.

I don't hear the bells when Allie gets married. She's too far away. She's gone down that highway – right through to the state of Texas. She becomes a first wife. In a brand new community of true believers, living the principle – at a ranch in the desert.

The night she told me she was leaving she was calm as a stone. Keeping sweet. Even with the fuss I was making.

Allie …

She's sitting right beside me, but she's a million miles away. She's already gone.

Blackout.

Part Four

GRACIE *is fifteen years old.*
It's fall.
Late morning.
GRACIE *is outside with* EMMA *and* JUSTIN.

Emma points from her stroller. She wants to know the name of everything she sees.

> *That's a pile of leaves. That's your brother Justin. That's the fence. And this here's the sweetest horse in all the world.*

Triumph pushes his forehead against my hand.

> *That's Triumph's way of saying hello. Hello Emma ...*

Justin looks Dancer over.

> *Dancer's ornery. But he's nice, deep down, once you get to know him. Just like you.*

This morning Justin got in trouble for throwing rocks at The Grannies. Mumma was having her night with Mr. Shelby so it was Mariah gave him a spanking. He would've thrown a rock at Mariah too if he had one handy.

The second we're in the door he tells Mumma what Mariah did. Mumma looks worn out again. We all wish she wouldn't have any more nights with Mr. Shelby. We worry about her getting pregnant. Marie worries about Mumma too, but she worries more about herself. She still isn't pregnant and her and Stanley have been married for over a year.

Mumma tells Justin that Mariah shouldn't have spanked him.

Well someone had to! You can't let him and his cousins throw rocks at a bunch of old women.

(*as* MUMMA) They've got no business marching around like that –

I don't like The Grannies any more than you do ... Did you tell him to throw those rocks? Mumma – you didn't!

Now Mumma's going on again about her mother.

(*as* MUMMA) When Grandma Lorraine was little, she sees a line of police cars coming closer and closer, winding down the road like a snake. Two-hundred sixty children loaded up and taken away. The parents locked up in jail.

Mumma pulls Justin close.

(*as* MUMMA) How'd you feel if I got sent to jail and you had to go live with another family in a strange city for two years? I guess Gracie's got no problem with that.

Go lie down. You look tired Mumma.

She says she's just fine. But she heads into her bedroom anyway.

Justin looks scared to death.

That raid when Grandma Lorraine got taken was fifty years ago. In America. That's not going to happen here. We've got rights. Mumma's not going anywhere and neither are you.

Beat.

I take Emma out in the stroller again. It's started to snow.

That's your mittens. That's a puddle. That's your sweet little hat in the puddle. This is the last time I'm picking it up ...

We get to Celeste's house. Her van's gone. I can't help myself. I knock on the door.

Amanda answers. Roberta drags Jamie-Junior on a towel behind her. And I feel better, just like that. Celeste didn't run away today. She'd never leave her kids.

Beat.

Mr. Shelby, Marie, and Stanley are sitting around the table, drinking apple cider. I get Emma settled in the bedroom. Mumma sends Justin back outside to play.

(*as* SHELBY) Gracie.

Mr. Shelby stands up. He wants me to sit between Marie and Stanley. He's had a dream that wasn't a regular dream. It was a vision that came from God – a revelation. He saw Stanley. And he saw me. Our children between us, at Heaven's door.

Stanley reaches for my hand. Marie reaches for my other hand. And the three of us are joined together.

(*as* SHELBY) You'll be a true sister to your sister Marie in every way.

Marie doesn't look at me. She looks down at my hand that's inside her hand. Stanley's hand is soft and warm and heavy. Like him.

Mumma ...

She's at the stove; she picks up the cider pot. I shut my eyes and ask God for strength. Now Stanley's hand is all slippery with sweat. And just like that, I'm out the door.
Mumma and her cider pot follow me out to the porch.

(*as* MUMMA) What do you think you're doing? Get back in there! Apologize to both of them. And to Marie.

I can't do it. I don't want to marry Stanley. He's an old man. I'm not good like Marie. I don't want to marry anyone. Not yet.

Mumma grabs hold of my arm. I try and pull away. And Mumma tries to pull me back.
Cider flies out of the pot. It splashes on my throat, then runs down inside my dress.

(*as* MUMMA) Gracie ...

The burn is alive and it isn't alive, all at the same time. Mumma scrapes up snow from the porch.

(*as* MUMMA) This is going to help.

Mr. Shelby comes out.

(*as* MUMMA) We had a little accident. Gracie got burnt.

He watches Mumma pack snow down between my dress and underthings. Mumma asks if that's better.

> *Better.*

He tells Mumma to go back inside.

(*as* SHELBY) You shouldn't be out in the cold.

He gives Mumma a hand up.

(*as* SHELBY) Go back in.

I don't know how I didn't see it before. She's pregnant again.
    Mumma looks at me. And she looks at him.

> *Mumma …*

She goes back in.
    My hands are shaking. When I try and stand, the world turns upside down on me.
    He wants to know if there's something I want to say to him.

> *I can't marry Stanley.*

Mr. Shelby knows I'm nervous. That's normal.

I don't feel normal. I feel terrible.

He says there's no rush. Stanley will be patient with me.

*Why couldn't you be patient with Mumma? Maybe you're
mixed up between what God wants and what you want.
Maybe that's why eight of your wives ran away.*

The door slams shut.
    The wind stirs up the trees. What on earth ... Now
something rustles from underneath. The Devil come for
me at last.
    Justin pulls himself up from under the porch.

You're not supposed to play down there.

He wants to know where I'm going.

I don't know. Go back in the house.

For once he doesn't argue with me.

        GRACIE *walks slowly.*

I pass by the school. "Keep sweet" in white stones out front.
I look beyond the chain. The Grannies have been protesting
all week but now the road is empty. I go by Celeste's. Her
van's still gone.

        Beat.

I don't remember climbing up the path. I sit on a stump, rest my head on the hubcap table. I pack snow on the burn, the way Mumma did …

GRACIE lies down.

Jesus lays me down to sleep, on the little mattress covered in moss …

Lights shift.
GRACIE sleeps. Snow falls.

I dream Goldfish crackers … float down from the sky. And that Marie's beside me … taking all the covers.

GRACIE wakes up.

Our Saviour lasted forty days in the desert. I couldn't last four hours.

GRACIE stands with difficulty.

Jesus makes the moon bright. He keeps me away from the patches of ice. I let Him show me the way, one step at a time. Down the mountain. On to the main road. He leaves me at the metal steps, outside the fall-down trailer. Before I can figure out why He would take me there, a door opens …

I don't know the boy that opens the door, but he knows me. He says Billy hasn't lived here in years.

I know.

Last he heard Billy was in Nelson – the town where the hippies live. The boy reaches for his own throat.

(*as THE BOY*) Hey, what happened to you?

And I suppose I faint.

Blackout.

Part Five

One day later.
GRACIE is in the hospital.

The nurse says I'm lucky the burn is first degree. I don't feel lucky. Every time someone comes in the room I ask if they've heard from Mumma. In the morning a nurse finally says my family's coming to get me. She gives me ointment and gauze to take with me. She shows me how to keep things clean. She asks me what grade I'm in.

Tenth grade.

She knows most of us don't go beyond grade ten. She grew up in our community and hopes I'll come into town for grade eleven and twelve.

I will.

Then she slips five dollars into my hand to get something nice at the gift store. And I feel guilty for lying. I'm going to quit school next month, the second I turn sixteen.

(*as THE NURSE*) Do you need someone to talk to, Gracie?

No thank you, I don't.

I buy some markers for Emma. The purple one smells like blueberries. I go back to my room and wait for Mumma. Or maybe it'll be Mariah. Or Kathleen or Rita.

Beat.

It's not Mumma. His long hair is gone. Shaved right off. He doesn't have any hair at all except for a little beard. Monster tattoos cover both his arms.

What are you doing here?

(*as BILLY*) Nice to see you too, Gracie.

Billy plops a garbage bag down in front of me. The things from my two drawers are inside.

(*as BILLY*) She left that out on the porch.

Did you talk to Mumma? What'd she say? Tell me!

(*as BILLY*) She don't want you back.

I pick up the bag and start down the hall. It's snowing again.

Do you have a car? He points to a muddy old thing on the edge of the parking lot. I'd appreciate a ride home.

He lights a cigarette.

(*as BILLY*) You're not going home. You're coming with me.

I'm going home whether or not it's you that gets me there.

(*as BILLY*) Then I'll call Child Services. And they'll call the police. Lock up the whole bunch, including Mumma. That's fine with me.

He hands me a letter addressed to the United States of America. Mumma prints like someone eight years old. She gives Billy permission to take me across the border.

"To William Owen Jenkins" ...

Billy looks pleased as punch.

(*as BILLY*) That's our dad.

A birth certificate is attached to the letter. Grace Lorraine Jenkins ... The girl I used to be.

(*as BILLY*) That's Mumma's idea of looking out for you. Dropping you off with the daddy you never knew. At least we got an address now. He's got his own landscaping business in Las Vegas. I've been looking for him a long time.

I keep walking. First pay phone I see, I'll call Celeste and she'll come running.

I don't want nothing to do with him.

(*as BILLY*) In a couple of weeks you turn sixteen. Then you can go live on the moon if that's what you want. Until then, I'm responsible for you. And we're gonna go see our dad.

Then I've got an apprenticeship starting up, back home in Nelson. And you've got school.

I don't care about school.

(*as BILLY*) Maybe you should. Now get in the car.

The car sounds like a tractor. Billy says it's from Japan and that means it'll run forever. Billy's got his grade twelve finally. He's getting his pipefitter's ticket. He makes Nelson sound like the best place to live in all the world. He thinks he's some big success. Maybe he thinks I've turned nice all of a sudden. Maybe he thinks the fight's gone out of me. He doesn't know I'm making plans. He rolls the window down so he can blow smoke outside. Cold air fills up the car.
He says he'll do the talking at the border.

(*as BILLY*) Try looking normal.

I'll turn around and walk back to Mumma. I'll ask her to forgive me … The border man waves us through.
I shut my eyes. When I wake up the mountains aren't close anymore and the road is straight and wide. The sun goes down and cold air fills up the car again. I'll go to Allie in Texas. Soon as I get enough money for a bus.
Billy hardly lets me out of his sight. He knows I want to run away. We don't sleep in tents. We sleep in motels – the Super 8 and the Country Hide-Away. The Super 8 isn't eight dollars; it's fifty-five dollars. And the Country Hide-Away isn't really hidden. We can hear the Interstate outside the door, all night long. Billy turns on the TV first thing, as soon as we're in the door.

I don't watch TV.

He turns up the sound – loud.

 I go in the bathroom. I clean the burn and put the ointment on – just like I'm supposed to. I hear a girl on the TV singing a song and then some people telling her what's wrong with how she sung it. Now someone sings "Jesus Take the Wheel." I take a peek – a little, tiny girl in a little, tiny dress. I watch some TV and then some more. We end up watching it until four a.m. both nights. I've never been up that late before. I could've watched the TV all night, but Billy made me go to bed so we wouldn't sleep through checkout and have to pay more money.

Beat.

The third day we come to a set of traffic lights.

(*as* BILLY) We're taking a detour.

As soon as he makes the turn I know where we are and where we're going. We drive through mountains, burnt by the sun. No trees, no snow yet neither.

Beat.

There're more houses than I remember. A lot of them are boarded up. A water tower, a playground.

We weren't allowed to ride our bikes no more … I had to ride my bike to that playground and leave it on a big pile of bikes. Marie thought they sold our bikes to some other kids. Celeste said they lit them on fire.

(*as* BILLY) It was crazy here, right before we moved up to Canada. New rule every day. It was good – way before that though – when we lived there.

Billy points to a little square house.

(*as* BILLY) That's the house our dad built. You made noise all day in your high chair, in this made-up language. Dad thought you were part Chinese …

Across the street is Cyrus's big house. It's not as grand as I remember. The yard where we listened to the prophet on tape is covered with tires and rusted-out things …

Cyrus was a funny old man.

Beat.

(*as* BILLY) They don't put you in jail for being funny. I remember what happened here. None of it was Dad's fault.

He killed our dog on purpose.

(*as* BILLY) You're just saying what Mumma says.

It still isn't right.

(*as* BILLY) Neither is assigning your wife and kids to the old bugger across the street. Dad loses the house he built and paid a mortgage on. Everything goes to the prophet. He was just trying to get out of the driveway before they took his truck too and Sammy got in the way. He loved Sammy. He loved all of us – including you. Don't have some big chip on your shoulder when you meet him. Give Dad a chance.

You just want to get rid of me.

(*as* BILLY) Now you're being ignorant.

I hate it here.

(*as* BILLY) It's where we were born. Where Mumma and her Mumma were born too. They've been doing the same math around here for a hundred years. It all comes down to math.

I hate math. You know that.

(*as* BILLY) If a man's got thirty wives – including the one he took from you – that's twenty-nine guys who don't have no wife at all. What's the value of a guy with no wife? Zero. That leaves a lot of guys with no place to call home. A lot of boys living in the woods.

It's better living in Canada. Better than here.

(*as* BILLY) Different place, same old story.

Beat.

We go back to the highway. Signs tell us how close we're getting – mile this and mile that. And what a good time we're going to have when we get there. "What happens in Vegas stays in Vegas." That doesn't make any more sense than what we saw on the TV these last two nights.

Do you still believe in God?

Billy says it isn't anyone's business what he believes.
He reaches for his lighter.

Cigarettes are bad for you. It doesn't matter what you believe to know that's true.

(*as BILLY*) Telling people what's good or bad for them is worse than smoking …

I ask him about Vancouver and he tells me that's the place he got clean and sober, end of story.

Mumma's pregnant again.

(*as BILLY*) Of course she is.

She almost died having Emma … They wanted me to marry Stanley. Your old foreman. He's already married to Marie.

(*as BILLY*) Son of a bitch. You can stay with me long as you want. I got a little room, used to be for junk. I already put a bed in there.

And all of a sudden Las Vegas rises up from the desert, all wavy in the sun. "Light comprehendeth all things." And I know. I know I'm never going home.

Beat.

We find a motel right across from a mall. Desert Dream. Maybe I'm in a dream. We go to Walmart. Billy wants me to get some normal clothes, anything I want. I find a dress covered in little pink flowers.

(*as* BILLY) That's not a dress; it's a nightgown. A nightgown an old lady would wear.

I get a jean skirt. A top with a drawing of a bird. Billy says to try on the new clothes. I want to go back to the motel and try them on in the bathroom there.

(*as* BILLY) You've got to try stuff on before you buy it.

A lady – behind a counter, at the change rooms – looks at my skirt and top. She gives me a plastic card with a number two. There's no numbers on the doors. I try the second one and someone inside there gets mad at me.
  I tell the lady that the change room two doors down's got someone inside.

(*as* WALMART CLERK) Then don't go in it.

She thinks I'm dumb as a post. That's for certain.

(*as WALMART CLERK*) Girl, go into a fitting room with a door that's open.

GRACIE finds an open door; the brightly lit
fitting room. She looks at herself in the mirror.

This is where I end up. I end up here.

Mirrors twice the size of me, front and back …

Lights bright enough to make you blink. "The body which is filled with light comprehendeth all things."

My dress looks terrible even though I tried to wash it in the sink last night. Runners covered in dried-up mud. I'm surprised they let me in the door at Walmart.

GRACIE watches herself in the mirror,
carefully slides both arms out of her dress.

The burn doesn't burn no more. The pain's gone inside.
At night it makes me go still; hold myself tight from head to toe. I pretend Marie's there snoring, so I can fall asleep.
But the pain doesn't let me sleep. It's not from the burn.
It's from losing Mumma – losing Marie and Celeste, Justin and Emma …

GRACIE slowly lowers her dress until it pools
around her feet. She wears her undergarments,
unravels her braid, makes a sorrowful
sound, and sinks down to the floor.

Someone's knocking on the door. The lady from the counter wants to know if I need assistance.

I need my brother.

Billy comes. He sits down on the floor beside me.

(*as BILLY*) Hush, hush. Hush now.

I don't want to wear the new clothes! Not yet ...

(*as BILLY*) Okay. You set the pace.

Billy puts his hand on my back. He puts his other arm around me. And the pain flattens out, just a little ...
    I start to float ... I rise up above the pain ... Higher and higher ... The air is blue and full of spirits ... I look down and see myself, there on the floor with Billy. The pain becoming small as a seed. Then I float up so high I can't see myself no more.
    I see our duplex, Emma's stroller out on the porch. The fall-down trailer out beyond the chain. Then I see Mumma weeding in the front field. Marie working in the kitchen. Celeste with a little one on her hip and Roberta pulling her brother in a wagon. I pray for Jesus to watch over them. Each and every one. Watch over me and Billy. Watch over our daddy. Help us know him again.
    Then I'm back there on the floor, inside Billy's skinny arms.

Beat.

Tell me what your apartment looks like.

He says it's old but he's been fixing it up. You can see the lake out the kitchen window if you stand on your tippy-toes.

I shut my eyes.

I see that lake.

Billy asks me if I'm ready to stand up now. He gets up first. He reaches down with both his hands.

I'm ready.

Blackout.
End of play.

NOTES ON SOURCES

On pages 21 and 28 of this book, Gracie misquotes Section 88:7–9 of the Mormon text *The Doctrine and Covenants*. On page 26, Gracie quotes Section 88:45 of the same book, and on pages 54 and 55, she quotes Section 88:67.

Sources and suggestions for further reading include the following:

Bramham, Daphne. *The Secret Lives of Saints: Child Brides and Lost Boys in Canada's Polygamous Mormon Sect.* Toronto: Vintage Canada, 2009.

Church of Jesus Christ of Latter-day Saints, The. *The Doctrine and Covenants*, §88. *The Church of Jesus Christ of Latter-day Saints.* Accessed February 2018. https://www.lds.org/scriptures/dc-testament/dc/88.

Dachsel, Marita. *Glossolalia.* Vancouver: Anvil Press, 2013.

Ebershoff, David. *The 19th Wife.* New York: Random House, 2009.

Jessop, Carolyn, and Laura Palmer. *Escape.* New York: Broadway Books, 2007.

Krakauer, Jon. *Under the Banner of Heaven: A Story of Violent Faith.* New York: Anchor Books, 2004.

Measom, Tyler, and Jennilyn Merten, dir. *Sons of Perdition.* 2010; United States: Left Turn Films, 2011. DVD, 85 min.

Palmer, Debbie, and Dave Perrin. *Keep Sweet: Children of Polygamy.* Lister, British Columbia: Dave's Press, 2004.

ACKNOWLEDGMENTS

I am very grateful to the Belfry Theatre in Victoria, British Columbia, which commissioned *Gracie*. Thank you to both the Belfry and co-producer Alberta Theatre Projects (ATP) for the extended rehearsal schedule and workshops, for our long history of working together, and for supporting Canadian playwrights. Thank you to the Banff Centre and Tamara Ross. Daphne Bramham's book *The Secret Lives of Saints* was an essential resource in creating this play, as were Jon Krakauer's *Under the Banner of Heaven* and Marita Dachsel's *Glossolalia*. Thank you to Celine Stubel. Thank you first readers Dede Crane, Don Hannah, Bill Gaston, Ken Garnhum, and, again, Marita Dachsel.

Vanessa Porteous wrangled *Gracie* out of my head and onto the stage. She read too many drafts and gave insightful, thorough, and challenging notes – as did Michael Shamata and Ivan Habel. They also assembled a remarkable team to work on *Gracie*; thank you to Catherine, Narda, Tobin, Jen, Sadie, and Meredith. Lili – you were a wonder from day one, and helped so much with the creation of *Gracie* – thank you. Premiering at home for the first time, at the Belfry, with all of you, was a gift in every way. I'm feeling it …

JOAN MACLEOD's plays include *Jewel; Toronto, Mississippi; Amigo's Blue Guitar; The Hope Slide; Little Sister; 2000; The Shape of a Girl; Homechild; Another Home Invasion;* and *The Valley.* She also wrote a libretto for a chamber opera – an adaptation of the classic children's novel *The Secret Garden.* Her work has been translated into eight languages. She is the recipient of numerous awards including two Floyd S. Chalmers Canadian Play Awards, the Governor General's Literary Award for English Language Drama, and in 2011 she received the Siminovitch Prize in Theatre. For seven years she was a playwright-in-residence at Toronto's Tarragon Theatre. Joan also writes poetry, prose, and for television. Since 2004, she has worked at the University of Victoria as a Professor in the Department of Writing. In 2016, she became a Fellow of the Royal Society of Canada.